CONTACT INFORMATION	
NAME	
ADDRESS	
PHONE #	
EMAIL	

DEDICATION

This Metal Detecting Log is dedicated to all the metal detectorists who want to record and retain information while out searching for treasures.

You are my inspiration for producing this book and I'm honored to be a part of helping you manage and retain important information regarding your metal detecting.

HOW TO USE THIS BOOK

This Metal Detecting Log Book will help you record, collect, and organize your information in an easy to use format.

Here are examples of information for you to fill in and write the details for treasure hunts.

Fill in the following information:

1. 100 Metal Detecting Log Pages
2. Record - Date, Time, Location, GPS, Machine Used, Machine Settings
3. Record - Item, Condition, and Estimated Value

METAL DETECTING LOG SHEET

DATE		TIME	
LOCATION			
GPS			
MACHINE USED			
MACHINE SETTINGS			

ITEM	CONDITION	EST. VALUE

METAL DETECTING LOG SHEET

DATE		TIME	
LOCATION			
GPS			
MACHINE USED			
MACHINE SETTINGS			

ITEM	CONDITION	EST. VALUE

METAL DETECTING LOG SHEET

DATE		TIME	
LOCATION			
GPS			
MACHINE USED			
MACHINE SETTINGS			

ITEM	CONDITION	EST. VALUE

METAL DETECTING LOG SHEET

DATE		TIME	
LOCATION			
GPS			
MACHINE USED			
MACHINE SETTINGS			

ITEM	CONDITION	EST. VALUE

METAL DETECTING LOG SHEET

DATE		TIME	
LOCATION			
GPS			
MACHINE USED			
MACHINE SETTINGS			

ITEM	CONDITION	EST. VALUE

METAL DETECTING LOG SHEET

DATE		TIME	
LOCATION			
GPS			
MACHINE USED			
MACHINE SETTINGS			

ITEM	CONDITION	EST. VALUE

METAL DETECTING LOG SHEET

DATE		TIME	
LOCATION			
GPS			
MACHINE USED			
MACHINE SETTINGS			

ITEM	CONDITION	EST. VALUE

METAL DETECTING LOG SHEET

DATE		TIME	
LOCATION			
GPS			
MACHINE USED			
MACHINE SETTINGS			

ITEM	CONDITION	EST. VALUE

METAL DETECTING LOG SHEET

DATE		TIME	
LOCATION			
GPS			
MACHINE USED			
MACHINE SETTINGS			

ITEM	CONDITION	EST. VALUE

METAL DETECTING LOG SHEET

DATE		TIME	
LOCATION			
GPS			
MACHINE USED			
MACHINE SETTINGS			

ITEM	CONDITION	EST. VALUE

METAL DETECTING LOG SHEET

DATE		TIME	
LOCATION			
GPS			
MACHINE USED			
MACHINE SETTINGS			

ITEM	CONDITION	EST. VALUE

METAL DETECTING LOG SHEET

DATE		TIME	
LOCATION			
GPS			
MACHINE USED			
MACHINE SETTINGS			

ITEM	CONDITION	EST. VALUE

METAL DETECTING LOG SHEET

DATE		TIME	
LOCATION			
GPS			
MACHINE USED			
MACHINE SETTINGS			

ITEM	CONDITION	EST. VALUE

METAL DETECTING LOG SHEET

DATE		TIME	
LOCATION			
GPS			
MACHINE USED			
MACHINE SETTINGS			

ITEM	CONDITION	EST. VALUE

METAL DETECTING LOG SHEET

DATE		TIME	
LOCATION			
GPS			
MACHINE USED			
MACHINE SETTINGS			

ITEM	CONDITION	EST. VALUE

METAL DETECTING LOG SHEET

DATE		TIME	
LOCATION			
GPS			
MACHINE USED			
MACHINE SETTINGS			

ITEM	CONDITION	EST. VALUE

METAL DETECTING LOG SHEET

DATE		TIME	
LOCATION			
GPS			
MACHINE USED			
MACHINE SETTINGS			

ITEM	CONDITION	EST. VALUE

METAL DETECTING LOG SHEET

DATE		TIME	
LOCATION			
GPS			
MACHINE USED			
MACHINE SETTINGS			

ITEM	CONDITION	EST. VALUE

METAL DETECTING LOG SHEET

DATE		TIME	
LOCATION			
GPS			
MACHINE USED			
MACHINE SETTINGS			

ITEM	CONDITION	EST. VALUE

METAL DETECTING LOG SHEET

DATE		TIME	
LOCATION			
GPS			
MACHINE USED			
MACHINE SETTINGS			

ITEM	CONDITION	EST. VALUE

METAL DETECTING LOG SHEET

DATE		TIME	
LOCATION			
GPS			
MACHINE USED			
MACHINE SETTINGS			

ITEM	CONDITION	EST. VALUE

METAL DETECTING LOG SHEET

DATE		TIME	
LOCATION			
GPS			
MACHINE USED			
MACHINE SETTINGS			

ITEM	CONDITION	EST. VALUE

METAL DETECTING LOG SHEET

DATE		TIME	
LOCATION			
GPS			
MACHINE USED			
MACHINE SETTINGS			

ITEM	CONDITION	EST. VALUE

METAL DETECTING LOG SHEET

DATE		TIME	
LOCATION			
GPS			
MACHINE USED			
MACHINE SETTINGS			

ITEM	CONDITION	EST. VALUE

METAL DETECTING LOG SHEET

DATE		TIME	
LOCATION			
GPS			
MACHINE USED			
MACHINE SETTINGS			

ITEM	CONDITION	EST. VALUE

METAL DETECTING LOG SHEET

DATE		TIME	
LOCATION			
GPS			
MACHINE USED			
MACHINE SETTINGS			

ITEM	CONDITION	EST. VALUE

METAL DETECTING LOG SHEET

DATE		TIME	
LOCATION			
GPS			
MACHINE USED			
MACHINE SETTINGS			

ITEM	CONDITION	EST. VALUE

METAL DETECTING LOG SHEET

DATE		TIME	
LOCATION			
GPS			
MACHINE USED			
MACHINE SETTINGS			

ITEM	CONDITION	EST. VALUE

METAL DETECTING LOG SHEET

DATE		TIME	
LOCATION			
GPS			
MACHINE USED			
MACHINE SETTINGS			

ITEM	CONDITION	EST. VALUE

METAL DETECTING LOG SHEET

DATE		TIME	
LOCATION			
GPS			
MACHINE USED			
MACHINE SETTINGS			

ITEM	CONDITION	EST. VALUE

METAL DETECTING LOG SHEET

DATE		TIME	
LOCATION			
GPS			
MACHINE USED			
MACHINE SETTINGS			

ITEM	CONDITION	EST. VALUE

METAL DETECTING LOG SHEET

DATE		TIME	
LOCATION			
GPS			
MACHINE USED			
MACHINE SETTINGS			

ITEM	CONDITION	EST. VALUE

METAL DETECTING LOG SHEET

DATE		TIME	
LOCATION			
GPS			
MACHINE USED			
MACHINE SETTINGS			

ITEM	CONDITION	EST. VALUE

METAL DETECTING LOG SHEET

DATE		TIME	
LOCATION			
GPS			
MACHINE USED			
MACHINE SETTINGS			

ITEM	CONDITION	EST. VALUE

METAL DETECTING LOG SHEET

DATE		TIME	
LOCATION			
GPS			
MACHINE USED			
MACHINE SETTINGS			

ITEM	CONDITION	EST. VALUE

METAL DETECTING LOG SHEET

DATE		TIME	
LOCATION			
GPS			
MACHINE USED			
MACHINE SETTINGS			

ITEM	CONDITION	EST. VALUE

METAL DETECTING LOG SHEET

DATE		TIME	
LOCATION			
GPS			
MACHINE USED			
MACHINE SETTINGS			

ITEM	CONDITION	EST. VALUE

METAL DETECTING LOG SHEET

DATE		TIME	
LOCATION			
GPS			
MACHINE USED			
MACHINE SETTINGS			

ITEM	CONDITION	EST. VALUE

METAL DETECTING LOG SHEET

DATE		TIME	
LOCATION			
GPS			
MACHINE USED			
MACHINE SETTINGS			

ITEM	CONDITION	EST. VALUE

METAL DETECTING LOG SHEET

DATE		TIME	
LOCATION			
GPS			
MACHINE USED			
MACHINE SETTINGS			

ITEM	CONDITION	EST. VALUE

METAL DETECTING LOG SHEET

DATE		TIME	
LOCATION			
GPS			
MACHINE USED			
MACHINE SETTINGS			

ITEM	CONDITION	EST. VALUE

METAL DETECTING LOG SHEET

DATE		TIME	
LOCATION			
GPS			
MACHINE USED			
MACHINE SETTINGS			

ITEM	CONDITION	EST. VALUE

METAL DETECTING LOG SHEET

DATE		TIME	
LOCATION			
GPS			
MACHINE USED			
MACHINE SETTINGS			

ITEM	CONDITION	EST. VALUE

METAL DETECTING LOG SHEET

DATE		TIME	
LOCATION			
GPS			
MACHINE USED			
MACHINE SETTINGS			

ITEM	CONDITION	EST. VALUE

METAL DETECTING LOG SHEET

DATE		TIME	
LOCATION			
GPS			
MACHINE USED			
MACHINE SETTINGS			

ITEM	CONDITION	EST. VALUE

METAL DETECTING LOG SHEET

DATE		TIME	
LOCATION			
GPS			
MACHINE USED			
MACHINE SETTINGS			

ITEM	CONDITION	EST. VALUE

METAL DETECTING LOG SHEET

DATE		TIME	
LOCATION			
GPS			
MACHINE USED			
MACHINE SETTINGS			

ITEM	CONDITION	EST. VALUE

METAL DETECTING LOG SHEET

DATE		TIME	
LOCATION			
GPS			
MACHINE USED			
MACHINE SETTINGS			

ITEM	CONDITION	EST. VALUE

METAL DETECTING LOG SHEET

DATE		TIME		
LOCATION				
GPS				
MACHINE USED				
MACHINE SETTINGS				

ITEM	CONDITION	EST. VALUE

METAL DETECTING LOG SHEET

DATE		TIME	
LOCATION			
GPS			
MACHINE USED			
MACHINE SETTINGS			

ITEM	CONDITION	EST. VALUE

METAL DETECTING LOG SHEET

DATE		TIME	
LOCATION			
GPS			
MACHINE USED			
MACHINE SETTINGS			

ITEM	CONDITION	EST. VALUE

METAL DETECTING LOG SHEET

DATE		TIME	
LOCATION			
GPS			
MACHINE USED			
MACHINE SETTINGS			

ITEM	CONDITION	EST. VALUE

METAL DETECTING LOG SHEET

DATE		TIME	
LOCATION			
GPS			
MACHINE USED			
MACHINE SETTINGS			

ITEM	CONDITION	EST. VALUE

METAL DETECTING LOG SHEET

DATE		TIME	
LOCATION			
GPS			
MACHINE USED			
MACHINE SETTINGS			

ITEM	CONDITION	EST. VALUE

METAL DETECTING LOG SHEET

DATE		TIME	
LOCATION			
GPS			
MACHINE USED			
MACHINE SETTINGS			

ITEM	CONDITION	EST. VALUE

METAL DETECTING LOG SHEET

DATE		TIME	
LOCATION			
GPS			
MACHINE USED			
MACHINE SETTINGS			

ITEM	CONDITION	EST. VALUE

METAL DETECTING LOG SHEET

DATE			TIME	
LOCATION				
GPS				
MACHINE USED				
MACHINE SETTINGS				

ITEM	CONDITION	EST. VALUE

METAL DETECTING LOG SHEET

DATE		TIME	
LOCATION			
GPS			
MACHINE USED			
MACHINE SETTINGS			

ITEM	CONDITION	EST. VALUE

METAL DETECTING LOG SHEET

DATE		TIME	
LOCATION			
GPS			
MACHINE USED			
MACHINE SETTINGS			

ITEM	CONDITION	EST. VALUE

METAL DETECTING LOG SHEET

DATE		TIME	
LOCATION			
GPS			
MACHINE USED			
MACHINE SETTINGS			

ITEM	CONDITION	EST. VALUE

METAL DETECTING LOG SHEET

DATE		TIME	
LOCATION			
GPS			
MACHINE USED			
MACHINE SETTINGS			

ITEM	CONDITION	EST. VALUE

METAL DETECTING LOG SHEET

DATE		TIME	
LOCATION			
GPS			
MACHINE USED			
MACHINE SETTINGS			

ITEM	CONDITION	EST. VALUE

METAL DETECTING LOG SHEET

DATE		TIME	
LOCATION			
GPS			
MACHINE USED			
MACHINE SETTINGS			

ITEM	CONDITION	EST. VALUE

METAL DETECTING LOG SHEET

DATE		TIME	
LOCATION			
GPS			
MACHINE USED			
MACHINE SETTINGS			

ITEM	CONDITION	EST. VALUE

METAL DETECTING LOG SHEET

DATE			TIME	
LOCATION				
GPS				
MACHINE USED				
MACHINE SETTINGS				

ITEM	CONDITION	EST. VALUE

METAL DETECTING LOG SHEET

DATE		TIME	
LOCATION			
GPS			
MACHINE USED			
MACHINE SETTINGS			

ITEM	CONDITION	EST. VALUE

METAL DETECTING LOG SHEET

DATE		TIME	
LOCATION			
GPS			
MACHINE USED			
MACHINE SETTINGS			

ITEM	CONDITION	EST. VALUE

METAL DETECTING LOG SHEET

DATE		TIME	
LOCATION			
GPS			
MACHINE USED			
MACHINE SETTINGS			

ITEM	CONDITION	EST. VALUE

METAL DETECTING LOG SHEET

DATE		TIME	
LOCATION			
GPS			
MACHINE USED			
MACHINE SETTINGS			

ITEM	CONDITION	EST. VALUE

METAL DETECTING LOG SHEET

DATE		TIME	
LOCATION			
GPS			
MACHINE USED			
MACHINE SETTINGS			

ITEM	CONDITION	EST. VALUE

METAL DETECTING LOG SHEET

DATE		TIME	
LOCATION			
GPS			
MACHINE USED			
MACHINE SETTINGS			

ITEM	CONDITION	EST. VALUE

METAL DETECTING LOG SHEET

DATE		TIME	
LOCATION			
GPS			
MACHINE USED			
MACHINE SETTINGS			

ITEM	CONDITION	EST. VALUE

METAL DETECTING LOG SHEET

DATE		TIME	
LOCATION			
GPS			
MACHINE USED			
MACHINE SETTINGS			

ITEM	CONDITION	EST. VALUE

METAL DETECTING LOG SHEET

DATE		TIME	
LOCATION			
GPS			
MACHINE USED			
MACHINE SETTINGS			

ITEM	CONDITION	EST. VALUE

METAL DETECTING LOG SHEET

DATE		TIME	
LOCATION			
GPS			
MACHINE USED			
MACHINE SETTINGS			

ITEM	CONDITION	EST. VALUE

METAL DETECTING LOG SHEET

DATE		TIME	
LOCATION			
GPS			
MACHINE USED			
MACHINE SETTINGS			

ITEM	CONDITION	EST. VALUE

METAL DETECTING LOG SHEET

DATE		TIME	
LOCATION			
GPS			
MACHINE USED			
MACHINE SETTINGS			

ITEM	CONDITION	EST. VALUE

METAL DETECTING LOG SHEET

DATE		TIME	
LOCATION			
GPS			
MACHINE USED			
MACHINE SETTINGS			

ITEM	CONDITION	EST. VALUE

METAL DETECTING LOG SHEET

DATE		TIME	
LOCATION			
GPS			
MACHINE USED			
MACHINE SETTINGS			

ITEM	CONDITION	EST. VALUE

METAL DETECTING LOG SHEET

DATE		TIME	
LOCATION			
GPS			
MACHINE USED			
MACHINE SETTINGS			

ITEM	CONDITION	EST. VALUE

METAL DETECTING LOG SHEET

DATE		TIME	
LOCATION			
GPS			
MACHINE USED			
MACHINE SETTINGS			

ITEM	CONDITION	EST. VALUE

METAL DETECTING LOG SHEET

DATE		TIME	
LOCATION			
GPS			
MACHINE USED			
MACHINE SETTINGS			

ITEM	CONDITION	EST. VALUE

METAL DETECTING LOG SHEET

DATE		TIME	
LOCATION			
GPS			
MACHINE USED			
MACHINE SETTINGS			

ITEM	CONDITION	EST. VALUE

METAL DETECTING LOG SHEET

DATE		TIME	
LOCATION			
GPS			
MACHINE USED			
MACHINE SETTINGS			

ITEM	CONDITION	EST. VALUE

METAL DETECTING LOG SHEET

DATE			TIME	
LOCATION				
GPS				
MACHINE USED				
MACHINE SETTINGS				

ITEM	CONDITION	EST. VALUE

METAL DETECTING LOG SHEET

DATE		TIME	
LOCATION			
GPS			
MACHINE USED			
MACHINE SETTINGS			

ITEM	CONDITION	EST. VALUE

METAL DETECTING LOG SHEET

DATE		TIME	
LOCATION			
GPS			
MACHINE USED			
MACHINE SETTINGS			

ITEM	CONDITION	EST. VALUE

METAL DETECTING LOG SHEET

DATE		TIME	
LOCATION			
GPS			
MACHINE USED			
MACHINE SETTINGS			

ITEM	CONDITION	EST. VALUE

METAL DETECTING LOG SHEET

DATE		TIME	
LOCATION			
GPS			
MACHINE USED			
MACHINE SETTINGS			

ITEM	CONDITION	EST. VALUE

METAL DETECTING LOG SHEET

DATE		TIME	
LOCATION			
GPS			
MACHINE USED			
MACHINE SETTINGS			

ITEM	CONDITION	EST. VALUE

METAL DETECTING LOG SHEET

DATE		TIME	
LOCATION			
GPS			
MACHINE USED			
MACHINE SETTINGS			

ITEM	CONDITION	EST. VALUE

METAL DETECTING LOG SHEET

DATE		TIME	
LOCATION			
GPS			
MACHINE USED			
MACHINE SETTINGS			

ITEM	CONDITION	EST. VALUE

METAL DETECTING LOG SHEET

DATE		TIME	
LOCATION			
GPS			
MACHINE USED			
MACHINE SETTINGS			

ITEM	CONDITION	EST. VALUE

METAL DETECTING LOG SHEET

DATE		TIME	
LOCATION			
GPS			
MACHINE USED			
MACHINE SETTINGS			

ITEM	CONDITION	EST. VALUE

METAL DETECTING LOG SHEET

DATE		TIME	
LOCATION			
GPS			
MACHINE USED			
MACHINE SETTINGS			

ITEM	CONDITION	EST. VALUE

METAL DETECTING LOG SHEET

DATE		TIME	
LOCATION			
GPS			
MACHINE USED			
MACHINE SETTINGS			

ITEM	CONDITION	EST. VALUE

METAL DETECTING LOG SHEET

DATE		TIME	
LOCATION			
GPS			
MACHINE USED			
MACHINE SETTINGS			

ITEM	CONDITION	EST. VALUE

METAL DETECTING LOG SHEET

DATE		TIME	
LOCATION			
GPS			
MACHINE USED			
MACHINE SETTINGS			

ITEM	CONDITION	EST. VALUE

METAL DETECTING LOG SHEET

DATE		TIME	
LOCATION			
GPS			
MACHINE USED			
MACHINE SETTINGS			

ITEM	CONDITION	EST. VALUE

METAL DETECTING LOG SHEET

DATE		TIME	
LOCATION			
GPS			
MACHINE USED			
MACHINE SETTINGS			

ITEM	CONDITION	EST. VALUE

www.ingramcontent.com/pod-product-compliance
Lightning Source LLC
Chambersburg PA
CBHW052207090526
44583CB00017BA/2416